101 Coolest '.
Do in Great Britain

Introduction

So you're going to Great Britain, huh? You lucky lucky thing! You are sure in for a treat because England, Wales, and Scotland all have innumerable treasures, so whether you are on the hunt for historic sites, outdoor adventures, or culinary treats there is no chance of you being disappointed.

This guide will take you on a journey from the major cities like London, Edinburgh, Manchester, and Cardiff, through to beach towns and cities such as Brighton and Plymouth, as well as to places in the countryside.

In this guide, we'll be giving you the low down on:
- the very best things to shove in your pie hole, from where to have the best traditional afternoon tea, to places to enjoy fish and chips
- incredible festivals, whether you would like to party hard while listening to international bands or you would like to celebrate the literary accomplishments of Britain

- the coolest historical and cultural sights that you simply cannot afford to miss from medieval castles right through to contemporary art galleries
- the most incredible outdoor adventures, whether you want to have a white water rafting adventure in Wales, or you fancy going on a dog sledding ride
- the places where you can party like a local and make new friends
- and tonnes more coolness besides!

Let's not waste any more time – here are the 101 coolest things not to miss in Great Britain!

1. Party on the Isle of Wight for Bestival

There is no doubt that Great Britain has one of the very best summer festival cultures to be found anywhere, so there won't be any question of you being able to attend a festival, but instead which of the many festivals you should attend. For our money, Bestival, which is hosted annually on the Isle of Wight, is always a very special experience. The four day festival takes place in early September, and previous headliners have included Beastie Boys, Elton John, and Florence and the Machine.

(www.bestival.net)

2. Go Fossil Hunting on the Jurassic Coast

The Jurassic Coast is a World Heritage Site, a stretch of coastline that extends from Exmouth to Studland Bay. As you might have expected from the name, this part of the British south coast is particularly special because it spans a staggering 185 million years of geological history, and this makes it an exciting place to go fossil hunting. Searching for fossils is also a fantastic way of getting kids interested in history, geology, and nature in a fun and interactive way.

(http://jurassiccoast.org)

3. Skate in Front of Somerset House

Although many people choose to visit Britain in the summer months, when the local population tends to be more cheerful and there are more daylight hours, we think that London does Christmas festivities very well indeed. If you find yourself in the English capital in the run up to Christmas and you are looking for a fun activity, you should know that there are pop-up ice skating rinks all over London during this time, and the loveliest of them all is perched directly in front of Somerset House, a stunning Neoclassical building that overlooks the River Thames.

(Strand, London WC2R 1LA, www.somersethouse.org.uk)

4. Take in the View From the London Eye

London is a very beautiful city, but it's even more so when you manage to take in the city from a height. And what better way of doing so than by taking a ride on the London Eye? At the time that the giant Ferris Wheel was constructed, it was the tallest Ferris wheel in the whole world with a height of 135 metres. As you reach the highest point in the capsule, you can take in the whole city, from the business district of Canary Wharf to the stunning buildings of the Houses of Parliament.

(Lambeth, London SE1 7PB; www.londoneye.com)

5. Eat Cheddar Cheese in Cheddar

You have probably heard of Cheddar cheese before, and you have probably eaten it as well, but you haven't really eaten Cheddar cheese at its best until you have visited the town of Cheddar in Somerset. And if you visit the Cheddar Gorge Cheese Company, you can actually see the cheese being made right in front of you. The cheese is made by hand and matured inside cloth for up to 18 months. And don't forget to eat plenty of the good stuff!

(www.cheddargorgecheeseco.co.uk)

6. Slide Down World's Largest Slide Tunnel

If you fancy yourself as something of an adventurer, and you prefer adventures to ambling from museum to museum, one of the greatest things that you can do is take a ride on The Slide, which is the world's tallest and longest tunnel slide with a height of 178 metres. Your trip down the slide will take a total of 40 seconds, and in this time you'll be taken round sharp turns, and you'll end with a 50 metre straight finish as you crash to the ground.

(Queen Elizabeth Olympic Park, 3 Thornton St, London E20 2AD; http://arcelormittalorbit.com/whats-on/the-slide)

7. Sample a Malt at the Arran Distillery

It is no secret that Scotland is a nation of whisky lovers and that a great deal of great quality whisky is produced in the country. If you want to take your whisky appreciation to the next level, it can be a great idea to get to grips with the whisky making process at a distillery, and one of our favourites is the Arran Distillery on the Isle of Arran. The island has a long history of producing single malt whisky but had done so illegally until this distillery opened in 1995. *(The Distillery, Lochranza, Isle of Arran KA27 8HJ; www.arranwhisky.com)*

8. Feel the Fun of the Edinburgh Fringe Festival

Every August, the population of Edinburgh doubles. Why? The Edinburgh Fringe Festival. This is the largest Fringe festival to be found anywhere in the world, and it's the perfect place to catch an up and coming show, whether you're into stand-up, musicals, or physical theatre. At the same time as the Fringe Fest, there's also a film festival and a television festival, so this is 100% the place to be if you're interested in the arts. August also comes to life with lots of all-night parties at the various Fringe venues across the city. *(www.edfringe.com)*

9. Visit the Roman Baths of Bath

If you are interested in the history of Great Britain, there are plenty of museums where you can learn about the extended history of the country, but a place where you can actually see history come to life is at the Roman baths of a city called Bath in Somerset. The famous bathhouse there is a very well preserved building that was used by the Romans for bathing. The bathhouse is pumped full of water via natural hot springs, and there is also a museum on-site where you can learn more about this impressive structure. *(Stall St, Bath BA1 1LZ, www.romanbaths.co.uk)*

10. Sip on Welsh Craft Beer at Albion Ale House

If you are a beer lover, you are certainly in the right place, and one of our favourite places to sip on craft ales is in the quaint Welsh town of Conwy called Albion Ale House. This pub has been named as one of the world's best bars by The Guardian, and it's with good reason. The point of difference here is that all the beers served up are from local breweries so you'll get to experience a true taste of Wales.

(Chapel Street, Conwy LL32 8RF,

http://albionalehouse.weebly.com)

11. Walk Along the Pembrokeshire Coastal Path

Since Great Britain is an island nation surrounded by water, it's a really wonderful place to enjoy some breath taking coastal landscapes and breathe in the sea air. One of our favourite spots for doing this has to be the Pembrokeshire Coastal Path in south Wales. The coastal path is 299km long so you'll have to break it up into a number of days, but if you love walking, it's well worth making the effort. Along the path, you'll walk through quaint towns such as Tenby, Solva, and Newport.

12. Visit the 14th Century Castle Linked to Macbeth

If historic architecture is what does it for you, you will have plenty to explore during your time in Scotland, and we think that one of the most special castles has to be Cawdor Castle. The castle is not only a beautiful piece of Scottish architecture, but it will resonate with bibliophiles as it has a connection with Shakespeare's Macbeth. In the play, Macbeth is made the Thane of Cawdor. The castle also has beautiful gardens, some of which date back to the 17th century.

(Cawdor, Nairn IV12 5RD;

www.cawdorcastle.com/Home.aspx)

13. Hike Helvellyn in the Lake District

If nothing makes you happier than strapping on your hiking boots, get yourself over to the Lake District in Cumbria where there is a landscape that abounds with various walks. One of the more challenging hikes in the area is up Helvellyn, which is the highest point of the Helvellyn range with an elevation of 950 metres. The most popular route of ascent is via Striding Edge, which takes around five and a half hours to complete. Needless to say, the views are breath taking.

14. Indulge a Chocaholic at Cadbury World

When life fails you, chocolate is the answer, and when life is good to you, chocolate is the answer. This is why there is no bad day to visit Cadbury World in Birmingham. With 14 chocolate zones, there is lots to learn and endless ways to have fun. You can learn where cocoa beans come from and how chocolate is made, you can play in chocolate rain, and enjoy a 4D chocolate cinema experience.

(Linden Rd, Bournville, Birmingham B30 1JR;
www.cadburyworld.co.uk)

15. Go for a Punt in Oxford

If you find yourself in Oxford or Cambridge, one of the words you're likely to hear banded around is "punting". A punt is essentially a flat bottomed boat that is used to navigate small water channels, and they are very popular in these university towns. When you are in Oxford, a punt on the river is a great way of exploring the town in a different kind of way. You'll have a guide who will steer the boat for you, so you just have to sit back and enjoy.

16. Visit the Church That Inspired Bram Stoker

Almost everybody has at least heard of Bram Stoker's famous tale of Count Dracula. Well, while this is an East European tale, there is also a moment when Dracula comes ashore to the coast of Yorkshire in England in a town called Whitby and ascends the 199 steps of Whitby Abbey. Well, this abbey is no fiction and you can see it for yourself. The first monastery here was established in the mid 17th century, and overlooks the North Sea. It's an incredible sight at sunset.

(Abbey Ln, Whitby YO22 4JT, www.whitbyabbey.co.uk)

17. Get Fired Up at Up Helly Aa

Up Helly Aa is the general name for any of the fire festivals that take place in the wintertime in Scotland to mark the end of the Yule season. While you'll be able to find a few of these celebrations at the end of January, the most famous takes place annually in Lerwick in the Shetlands. You'll find fire lit torches being paraded on the street with thousands of people looking on, and this then extends into an all-night party.

(www.uphellyaa.org)

18. Tuck Into Incredible Seafood at the Hidden Hut, Truro

Since Britain is surrounded by ocean, you can expect to eat some of the most delicious seafood of your life on your holidays there, and one of our favourite seafood restaurants is called the Hidden Hut in Truro, a quaint coastal town in the county of Cornwall. This restaurant is in a wooden shed by the beach, but don't let that put you off. The fresh mackerel salad followed by Cornish ice cream is a lunch you won't forget in a hurry.

19. Enjoy the Fine White Sand of Eigg

If you are the kind of traveller who likes to get away from it all and just immerse yourself in natural beauty, it's imperative that you make at least a couple of trips away from the mainland. The Isle of Eigg is a veritable paradise, and the highlight has to be a stretch of beach on the north west side of the island called Laig Bay. From the look of the white sand, you might wonder whether you are really in Scotland. Alas, the nip in the air will remind you sooner rather than later.

20. Catch some Contemporary Dance at Sadler's Wells

Without a shadow of a doubt, London is one of the cultural centres of the world, and you'll find everything from dance to visual arts to jazz and everything in between. If dance is what does it for you, Sadler's Wells in the city centre is a theatre dedicated to this art form, with a leaning towards contemporary art forms, but you can also catch ballets here. Dance lovers need to keep up to date with their programme of events.
(Rosebery Ave, London EC1R 4TN, www.sadlerswells.com)

21. Watch a Live Football Match at Old Trafford

The people of Britain are mad for football, and you should do your very best to catch a game while you're in the country. The least that you can do is head to a pub where you can watch the match on a screen, but if you do have the opportunity, go to one of the stadiums and feel all the electricity of a live match. Old Trafford stadium is home to the home to the famous football team, Manchester United, so get tickets for this place if you possibly can.

(Sir Matt Busby Way, Stretford, Manchester M16 0RA, www.manutd.com/en/Visit-Old-Trafford.aspx)

22. Enjoy a Canoeing Trip in the Wye Valley

The River Wye, which passes through the English-Welsh border at the foot of Wales is the fifth longest river in Great Britain, which means that it's a great place to try out some river activities such as canoeing. If you find yourself to Hay-on-Wye, a picturesque riverside town, you'll find plenty of places where you can rent canoes and enjoy the calm waters of the river, whether you want to enjoy the waters for a couple of hours or a couple of days.

23. Discover Egyptian Artefacts at the Manchester Museum

Manchester is a city with many cultural attractions, and if you fancy a day of learning, you can't do better than the Manchester Museum, which is dedicated to archaeology, anthropology, and natural history, and contains a staggering 4.5 million artefacts. While you can find objects from all over the globe here, it's the selection of Egyptian items that really stand out. The animal mummies are particularly impressive.

(University Of Manchester, Oxford Rd, Manchester M13 9PL, www.museum.manchester.ac.uk)

24. Be Stunned by 13th Century Brecon Cathedral

You might think that a small town in mid Wales with a population of less than 8000 people wouldn't be a very exciting place to visit, but if you get the chance to visit

Brecon, we think you"ll have a whale of a time. The stand out attraction in the town is Brecon Cathedral, a beautiful 13th century church that was built in a Gothic style during the reign of King John. The acoustics inside the cathedral are spectacular so do catch one of their concerts if you can.

(Cathedral Close, Brecon LD3 9DP,
www.breconcathedral.org.uk)

25. Eat Incredible Farm Fare at L'Enclume

When you're on holiday, it's time to be decadent and indulge, and if you love nothing more than to eat in great restaurants, we'd love to recommend L'Enclume, a restaurant located in a small village called Cartmel in Cumbria. Despite the isolated location, the restaurant has earned two prestigious Michelin stars for its delicious farm to table fare. Menu highlights include aged veal in coal oil, and native lobster with broad beans and elderflower.

(Cavendish St, Cartmel, Grange-over-Sands LA11 6PZ;
www.lenclume.co.uk)

26. Wave a Rainbow Flag at Brighton Pride

Any LGBT visitors to Great Britain will find that this great land is one of the most gay friendly places on the planet. And while you might expect London to be the epicentre of gay culture in Britain, that accolade actually goes to the smaller beach city of Brighton. Brighton is spectacularly gay at any time of the year, but it's during Brighton Pride that it really comes to life. It takes place at the beginning of August each year, and culminates with a huge street parade and an incredible festival style concert.

(http://brighton-pride.org)

27. Step Back in Time at Castell Henllys

If you are something of a history buff, there is tonnes to explore across Britain, but if you'd like to explore local history in a more engaging way than walking through a stuffy museum, we think that Castell Henllys in Pembrokeshire, Wales will be right up your alley. This is a unique Iron Age fort that has been recreated with replica Iron Age roundhouses that are built on top of excavated remains that date back 2400 years. *(Meline SA41 3UR, www.pembrokeshirecoast.org.uk)*

28. Explore the Dramatic White Scar Cave

If you would like to explore a landscape that is a little out of the ordinary, be sure to head to the Yorkshire Dales National Park where you can explore the White Scar Cave, the largest public cave in all of the UK. It is possible to take a two hour tour that will allow you to explore all the crevices of this incredible cave system, including underground streams, thousands of stalactites, and even waterfalls.
(White Scar Cave, Ingleton, Carnforth LA6 3AW, www.whitescarcave.co.uk)

29. Stroll Through the Cambridge University Botanic Garden

When tourists visit Cambridge, the priority for many people is to stroll through the hallowed halls of the Cambridge university colleges. And while this is great to do, sometimes you also want to relax in greenery, and the Cambridge University Botanic Garden offers exactly that opportunity. Created in 1831, the 40 acres contain a plant collection of over 8000 species, a range of glasshouses, and a rock garden.

(1 Brookside, Cambridge CB2 1JE,
www.botanic.cam.ac.uk/Botanic/Home.aspx)

30. Get Your Photo Taken in a Red Phone Booth

The red phone booth is something really iconic that you can find on the streets of London, even though everyone has a mobile phone these days and they are hardly ever used. But this means that you won't be jostling for competition to get inside the booth to take the perfect red phone "yes, I'm in London" selfie.

31. Enjoy the Festival Spirit of Festival No. 6

If you are somebody who cannot get enough of summer festivals, Great Britain has one of the most incredible festival cultures on the face of the planet.

Everybody has heard of Glastonbury but if you would like to explore something that is more up-and-coming, you should know about Festival No. 6, which is hosted in Portmeirion in Wales every September. As well as great music artists, this festival is famous for its activities like trapeze lessons and urban sketching. *(http://festivalnumber6.com)*

32. Ride the Rapids of the Cardiff International White Water Course

You might not think of a capital city such as Cardiff as a place where you can enjoy outdoor adventures, but that is not the case. At least not if you find your way to the Cardiff International White Water Course, because this is an Olympic standard centre of white water that offers some of the best white water rafting and canoeing that you can experience in the country. *(Watkiss Way, Cardiff CF11 0SY, www.wmc.org.uk)*

33. Have a Hiking Adventure up Ben Nevis

All adventure travellers have surely heard about Ben Nevis, which is the tallest mountain in all of Great Britain, standing tall at a height of 1345 metres above sea level. Located in the Highland town of Fort William, Ben Nevis is by no means an easy breezy walk. But if you are well versed in hiking and climbing, ascending this beast is an experience you won't forget in a hurry. And remember to wrap up warm!

34. Scale the Roof of the O2 Arena

When major international music artists come to London, there is one venue where they are sure to play, and that is the O2 Arena in the east part of the city. But many people don't realise that there's way more to do at this arena than just watching concerts. And for all outdoor adventurers, something you shouldn't skip is the opportunity to scale the dome of the arena. The highest point is 52 metres, and you can see for 15 miles around when you are at the peak.

(Peninsula Square, London SE10 0DX; www.theo2.co.uk)

35. Have Sunday Lunch to Remember in Sticky Walnut, Chester

Great Britain has not earned a reputation for being one of the most exciting culinary destinations on the planet, but we think this is unfair, particularly when it comes to traditional Sunday lunch, which is typically some kind of roasted meat served with roast potatoes, Yorkshire puddings, veggies, and gravy. It's comfort food at its best, and we love it at the Sticky Walnut in Chester, which includes roast beef with buttered kale and honey glazed carrots.

(11 Charles St, Chester CH2 3AZ; www.stickywalnut.net)

36. Enjoy the Pristine Beach of Lulworth Cove

Although Great Britain is a country that is totally surrounded by water, there are not very many people that visit with the express purpose of lazing on the beach. While it's true that the weather may not always be conducive to lazy beach days, the number of picturesque beaches you can find all over the country are very impressive indeed. Lulworth cove in Dorset is a firm favourite of ours. The cove is backed by tall cliffs, and the water is safe for swimming.

37. Get Lost in Ancient History at the British Museum

London is a museum lover's paradise. While you could easily spend a whole vacation making your way from one museum to another, if you only have time to fit one museum into your schedule, make sure that it's the British Museum. The history of this museum dates right back to the 18th century, and its exhibitions relating to ancient history are particularly impressive. Some special artefacts include a gold bowl from Sicily dated to 600 BC, and a beaded necklace from Scotland that dates to 3000 BC.

(Great Russell St, London WC1B 3DG; www.britishmuseum.org)

38. Visit the Spectacular Winchester Cathedral

For fans of religious architecture, a visit to the spectacular Winchester Cathedral is an absolute must use this is one of the largest and grandest cathedrals to be found anywhere in Europe. The first church on the site was built all the way back in 642, with most of the current cathedral structure dating back to the 12th century. As well as a stunning structure, there's also a great deal of art work inside the cathedral, including a piece by Antony Gormley. *(9 The Cl, Winchester SO23 9LS, www.winchester-cathedral.org.uk)*

39. Discover Prehistoric Scotland

If you make it to the Shetland Islands, as you absolutely should, you can find a prehistoric site whose history extends back to 2700BC. Jarlshof is really spectacular because there is evidence of 4000 years of history at this one site. You will be able to see Iron Age wheelhouses, Norse long houses, a medieval farmstead, and a rich collection of ancient artefacts in the visitor's centre.

(Sumburgh Head, Shetland ZE3 9JN; www.shetland-heritage.co.uk/jarlshof)

40. Get Literary in Poet's Corner of Westminster Abbey

Westminster Abbey is one of the must visit historic buildings of London. There is much to explore around the building, and literary types should not fail to visit Poet's Corner within the monastery. There are a huge number of writers, poets, and playwrights commemorated there, including notable figures such as Geoffrey Chaucer, Elizabeth Gaskell, C.S Lewis, and Ted Hughes.

(20 Deans Yd, Westminster, London SW1P 3PA, www.westminster-abbey.org)

41. Enjoy the Rides of Blackpool Pleasure Beach

Travelling with children has both rewards and challenges. Of course, it's wonderful to give your kids the opportunity to see different parts of the world but you also need to make sure they are kept entertained around the clock, which is easier said than done. One place where the kids are sure to have a smile on their faces is at Blackpool Pleasure Beach in the north of England. This is an amusement park located along the Blackpool coast, famous for its traditional wooden rollercoaster.

(525 Ocean Blvd, Blackpool FY4 1EZ,
www.blackpoolpleasurebeach.com)

42. Indulge in Oysters on the Isle of Mull

If you are a fan of seafood, you'll know that the best seafood has to be eaten fresh, and it doesn't get much fresher than the sea treats found on the Isle of Mull, where fishing is one of the main industries of the island, which is surrounded by nutrient rich waters. The Isle of Mull is particularly famed for its incredible oysters. You can't go wrong sampling them at any restaurant or pub on the island, but we particularly like Am Birlinn, which specialises in local seafood.

(Dervaig, Tobermory, Isle of Mull PA75 6QS;
www.ambirlinn.com)

43. Enjoy a Game of Golf in St Andrews

If your idea of a perfect getaway is packing up your golf clubs and hitting a few balls, Scotland is the perfect holiday destination for you. While there are courses all over the country, the most renowned area for golf is St Andrews. There are seven golf courses in and around the city, but the most famous is certainly the Old Course. This course is actually one of the oldest in the world as it opened in 1552, and it was the first course where the standard 18 holes was created.

(The Links House, W Sands Rd, St Andrews KY16 9XL; www.standrews.com/Play/Courses/Old-Course)

44. Take the Family to Warwick Castle

The middle part of England is often ignored by tourists on a trip to the country, but it is full with incredible treasures that are well worth visiting. Warwick Castle is just one of these. This medieval castle was originally created by William the Conqueror all the way back in 1068, but the original motte and bailey structure was rebuilt in stone in the 12th century. Climb to the tops of the towers for spectacular views, and in the summertime don't miss the live jousting matches! *(Warwick CV34 4QU, www.warwick-castle.com)*

45. Stay on a Farm on the Isle of Wight

The Isle of Wight is an absolutely gorgeous island off the south coast of England with lots of greenery and nature. A wonderful way of having a slightly alternative stay on the Isle of Wight is to skip the hotels, guesthouses, and hostels, and stay on a farm instead. Nettlecombe Farm is a place on the island that offers exactly that opportunity. This farm has been owned by the same family for over a century, with alpacas, donkeys, goats, reindeer, and even an emu. *(Nettlecombe Ln, Whitwell, Ventnor PO38 2AF, https://nettlecombefarm.co.uk)*

46. Enjoy an Incredible Rave Up at Boomtown Fair

Winchester might be best known as the Anglo-Saxon capital of England and its beautiful cathedral, but it's also a place that's home to an absolutely banging festival called Boomtown Fair, which is hosted each year in mid August. This music and arts festival entertains around 60,000 people every year, with all kinds of music performances, as well as theatre, circus, and dance productions.

(www.boomtownfair.co.uk)

47. Get Your Fill of Modern Art at the Tate

If you are an artsy kind of person, you can truly fill your boots while in London because this city is absolutely bursting full of incredible galleries. While there are many art spaces to choose from, the Tate Modern is probably the most impressive of all the London galleries. You can find it within a disused power station on the Southbank, and the sheer scale of the place is breath taking. What's more, the permanent collection is totally free to peruse so this makes for a cheap afternoon out.

(Bankside, London SE1 9TG, www.tate.org.uk/visit/tate-modern)

48. Visit Caernarfon Castle in Wales

Without a doubt, Caernarfon Castle is one of the most impressive and imposing historic structures in Wales. Edward I built the castle in the 1280s, and the cost of the structure was 90% of the country's annual income at the time – a staggering amount! A great deal of the remaining structure is still intact, and it can take a whole day to explore the winding alleys and staircases to get to know it all.

(Castle Ditch, Caernarfon LL55 2AY, www.caernarfon-castle.co.uk)

49. Ride the Bluebell Railway, a Scenic Train Ride

Great Britain is a country that is very well connected by train lines, and not only is this a fast way of zipping around the country, it's also a way to see the scenic landscapes that roll by. We think that one of the best train rides that you can take in the whole country is the Bluebell Railway, which will take you from Lewes to East Grinstead, a short distance of just about 11 miles. Taking this train is like stepping back in time, because the stations are old fashioned, the staff are dressed up in anachronistic uniforms, and the carriages that puff along look as though they are from another century as well.

(www.bluebell-railway.co.uk)

50. Party in the Street for Notting Hill Carnival

Ever since 1966, the West Indian community has led a massive street party on the streets of Notting Hill called the Notting Hill carnival. This honestly might be the most fun weekend of the entire calendar year in London, as everybody is very welcome to join in with all the fun. Whether you want to dance on the street in the day time or party right throughout the night, you're very welcome to join in as little or as much as you would like. *(http://thelondonnottinghillcarnival.com)*

51. Eat the Very Best Ice Cream in Wales

Let's face it, the weather in Wales is never going to be so extremely hot that you need to cool yourself down with an ice cream sundae, but the ice cream is so phenomenal at Parisella's of Conwy that you'd be a fool not to indulge even if you are visiting in the bleak midwinter. This ice cream parlour was set up by Italians who emigrated to Wales, and it dates all the way back to 1949. There are more than fifty flavours to choose from, including salted caramel, amaretto, and black cherry.

(The Ice Cream Kiosk St, Lower Gate St, Conwy LL32 8AL; http://parisellasicecream.co.uk)

52. Discover Ancient Britain at Stonehenge

Stonehenge might just be the most iconic historic landmark in a country with no shortage of historic landmarks. This prehistoric monument can be found in Wiltshire, a ring of standing stones that archaeologists believe was constructed somewhere between 3000BC and 2000BC. Nobody can be exactly sure what this monument was used for, but there is suggestion that it could have been a burial ground as fragments of bone have also been found there.

(Amesbury, Salisbury SP4 7DE)

53. Enjoy a Drink With a View in Glasgow

Glasgow is a very charming city, but it's impossible to appreciate the full beauty of the city when you are simply walking around the streets, so why not explore one of the city's rooftop bars? Well, actually there is only one, and it is at The Carlton George hotel. The bar is located on the 7th floor so you have a lovely view over the city, and their food and drink is pretty great too. Their afternoon tea is a little over a tenner and offers incredible value that cannot be beaten.
(44 W George St, Glasgow G2 1DH; www.carlton.nl/en/hotel-george-glasgow)

54. Learn How to Surf in Newquay

When you think of places in the world with a great surfing culture, your mind might wander to faraway places like Hawaii or the Pacific coast of Mexico, but believe it or not there is also an exceptional surfing culture to be found in Great Britain, and specifically in the southern counties of Somerset and Cornwall. Newquay in Cornwall is a town bursting full of surfing schools where you can rent equipment and have lessons so you can ride the impressive waves of this part of England.

55. Cruise the Waters of Lake Windermere

Lake Windermere is the largest natural lake in all of England, a wonderfully peaceful place to relax and enjoy the water and the green landscapes. As such, this is a very popular summer holiday spot for local people as well as foreigners, but because the expanse of the lake is so great, the only way to really explore all of it is to take a lake cruise. Cruises can last up to three hours, and show you through wooded islands, mountains scenery, secluded bays, and lots more beauty besides.

56. Take in the Scenery of the Seven Sisters Cliffs

England is a country with some of the dramatic coastline in the world, and you can experience all the majesty of this for yourself by taking a trip to the Seven Sisters Cliffs in East Sussex. The features of these dramatic chalk cliffs were created all the way back in prehistoric times when land was submerged and the waves pushed the chalk to the surface. And now all these years since then, the cliffs make for wonderful coastal walks and photograph opportunities.

57. Stay Overnight in a Lighthouse

When you travel around a country, you probably stay in guesthouses, hotels, and hostels, or maybe you'll try a spot of Couchsurfing. But if you fancy staying somewhere a little more special than the average, etch a trip to the Rua Reidh Lighthouse, which stands at the entrance of Loch Ewe, into your travel diary. This is a functional lighthouse with rooms for guests. From your window, you have the opportunity to spot dolphins, sea eagles, otters, and even whales.

(Melvaig, Gairloch IV21 2EA;
https://stayatalighthouse.co.uk)

58. Have a Day at the Races at Royal Ascot

Horse racing in Britain is something that is very much associated with the upper classes of the country, so if you would like to have a fancy day out that you won't forget, a day at the races could be just the ticket. There are numerous racecourses dotted around, and one of the best known is Ascot in Berkshire, most famous for its Royal Ascot racing weekend, which dates back to 1711. At this event, all the women dress up, wear hats, and sip champagne while betting on the horses. *(High St, Ascot SL5 7JX, www.ascot.co.uk)*

59. Experience a Scottish Ceilidh at Ghillie Dhu

In Scottish Folklore, the Ghillie Dhu is the name for a male fairy, but say the word on the streets of Edinburgh and everyone will point you to the venue of the same name. Ghillie Dhu is the number one place to have a truly Scottish night out on the town. While you can eat dinner there, it is best known for its traditional ceilidhs, which is essentially a knees up with folk music, traditional dancing, and storytelling.

(2 Rutland St, Edinburgh EH1 2AD; http://ghillie-dhu.co.uk)

60. Feel Britain's History at Canterbury Cathedral

Simply put, Canterbury Cathedral is one of the largest and most important cathedrals to be found in the whole country, and so this makes it a must visit for fans of history and architecture. The church was first built in 597 but then completely rebuilt in the 11th century, which is the structure you can see today. Some of the stained glass windows can be dated all the way back to the 12th century, so looking at them is like looking at history right in front of you.

(Cathedral House, 11 The Precincts, Canterbury CT1 2EH, www.canterbury-cathedral.org)

61. Sip on Cocktails at Manchester's Dusk Til Pawn

As the second city of England, Manchester is all too often overlooked, but there is something for everyone is this dynamic city, not least the opportunity to sip on a cocktail or two. There are plenty of wonderful cocktail bars in all corners of Manchester, but our favourite has to be Dusk Til Pawn. This bar has been created with a speakeasy style, making it an awesome place to kick back and relax on any night of the week. We particularly like their take on an Old Fashioned, which contains ginger and marmalade.

(Northern Quarter, Manchester M1 1FB)

62. Take the Jack the Ripper Tour of Whitechapel

In the late 19th century, prostitutes working on the streets of East London were singled out by a serial killer who is still unidentified to this day, but who goes by the name of Jack the Ripper. If you'd like to know more about this grizzly figure and his effect on the capital, you should absolutely take the Jack the Ripper Walking Tour, which will walk you through the streets of Whitechapel where the murders took place.

(www.thejacktherippertour.com)

63. Have an Epic Time at Glastonbury Festival

Glastonbury Festival is the most iconic summer festival in the country, and it's with good reason. First of all, although the festival is hosted in the height of summer each year, it manages to attract a huge amount of rain so be prepared to get muddy. Secondly, it's the place that all the most iconic artists from around the world want to play. Previous headliners have included the likes of New Order, James Brown, Coldplay, Blur, and Leonard Cohen.

(www.glastonburyfestivals.co.uk)

64. Have a Family Day on Brighton Pier

Brighton is a coastal city, just one hour away from London, that is absolutely bursting with charm, and it gives the impression of how London might have been in the 1970s. One of the most charming aspects of Brighton has to be the enduringly popular pier, which is popular with travellers, families, and couples alike. On the pier you'll find funfair rides, amusements, and traditional bites to eat like good old fish and chips.

(Madeira Dr, Brighton BN2 1TW, http://brightonpier.co.uk)

65. Be Mesmerised by the Aysgarth Falls

If you are the kind of person who likes to immerse themselves in the beauty of nature while you're on holiday, Britain is a place with almost endless amounts of greenery. One of our favourite spots to simply relax and just enjoy what nature has to offer is Aysgarth Falls in the Yorkshire Dales. Although the falls are not particularly tall, the water tumbles over a number of natural steps, making it an extremely pleasant spot to while away some quiet hours.

(Aysgarth Falls National Park Centre, Aysgarth, Leyburn, Yorkshire, DL8 3TH)

66. Have a Traditional Tea at Betty's in Harrogate

One of the simple pleasures of travelling within Britain is the joy of settling down in a traditional tea shop and helping yourself to an afternoon tea. Of course, there are spots all over the country where you can do this, but for the old fashioned and authentic experience of the British country, head to Betty's in Harrogate. You'll be faced with towering plates of sandwiches, scones, cakes, and of course, tea.

(1 Parliament Street, Harrogate, Yorkshire; www.bettys.co.uk)

67. Have a Whale Watching Adventure

Did you know that the west coast of Scotland is one of the very best places for whale watching adventures in the world? The North Minch, a strait in north-west Scotland, is particularly rich in marine life, and it's here that you can find a number of whale watching opportunities through tour companies who will take you out on a boat and make sure that you are really close to all of the action. You might also see dolphins, porpoises, sharks, seals, and otters.

68. Walk the Spectacular Coastline of the Lizard Peninsula

If coastal walks do it for you, there's no shortage of great hikes that will fill your lungs with fresh sea air in Britain. Cornwall is a great place for coastal hiking, and the Lizard peninsula of the county in particular. This peninsula is well known for its beautiful geology, and for the rare plants that grow there. You'll also find dramatic bays, and quaint seafood restaurants where you can chow down on the local catch of the day.

69. Walk the Woods and Valleys of Wessex Ridgeway

If you're a country bumpkin at heart, there is no shortage of countryside to be explored in England, and many rural pathways from which you can explore the country. One of the most popular long distance paths is the Wessex Ridgeway, which is a 138 mile trail that runs from Marlborough in Wiltshire to Lyme Regis on the Dorset coast. You'll walk through many incredible landscapes, including the stark beauty of Salisbury Plain, through to woodlands with lots of wildlife.

70. Visit the Largest Medieval Cathedral in Northern Europe

York Minster is the ideal city to visit if you want a taste of historic England but you don't want to be

overwhelmed by a city of an enormous size. There are a number of historic attractions in York, and perhaps the most famous of them all is York Minster which happens to be the largest medieval cathedral in northern Europe. The whole church structure is well worth exploring but York is particularly well known for its stained glass, and many of the stained glass paintings in York Minster can be traced back to the 12th century. *(Deangate, York YO1 7HH,*
https://yorkminster.org/home.html)

71. Take in a Show at the Wales Millennium Centre

As the capital city of Wales, Cardiff offers plenty of opportunities to be entertained, and the best place to catch a show in the city is at the Wales Millennium Centre. There are a total of eight arts organisations in residence here, including the national orchestra and opera, dance, literature, and theatre companies, which means that whether you want to take in some contemporary dance or a grand opera, there will be something in the programme of events that you find appealing.

(Bute Pl, Cardiff Bay CF10 5AL, www.wmc.org.uk)

72. Eat a Bakewell Tart in Bakewell

If you have something of a sweet tooth, fear not because the British people are rather keen on sweet things too, and you'll discover this when you pop into any bakery or local teahouse. One of the most popular British desserts is called Bakewell Tart, and this actually originates from a town called Bakewell in Derbyshire. Of course, it's worth going to this town if you want to taste the real deal, which consists of a shortcrust pastry filled with jam, frangipane, and flaked almonds.

73. Tour a Lavish Manor House, Chatsworth House

England is a country with more than its fair share of stately homes, and visiting one of these can make you feel as though you have been transported to a completely different era. One of the grandest in

England is Chatsworth House, a stately home in Derbyshire that dates back to the mid-16th century. A tour through the house will allow you to explore local history, and you can also check out the incredible European art collection, which contains works from the Old Masters through to 21st century art pieces. *(Bakewell DE45 1PP; www.chatsworth.org)*

74. Try Your Hand at Skiing in Cairnwell

While it's true that many people go to Europe in the wintertime to enjoy skiing, you probably think of Switzerland or France as the primary skiing destinations. While these are great locations to hit the slopes, do not discount bonny Scotland. In Cairnwell, you'll actually find the largest ski centre in Scotland, where you can take lessons no matter your experience. *(Cairnwell, Braemar AB35 5XU; http://ski-glenshee.co.uk)*

75. Get Artsy at the Buxton Festival

There are things to enjoy during any of the seasons in Britain, but it's during the summer that you can catch

most of the festivals, and the annual Buxton Festival, which dates back to 1979, is one of the most special of these. This is primarily a festival of opera, music, and literary readings and talks, but encompasses many art forms. For arts lovers, this is one not to miss.
(www.buxtonfestival.co.uk)

76. Visit the First Ever Public Museum, The Ashmolean

The Ashmolean in Oxford is extremely important because it's the world's first ever university museum. If you are someone who relishes in learning new things, this is a place that you need to check out. The collections inside are extremely varied, so there is bound to be something that suits every kind of person. Some of the highlights include Picasso paintings, a collection of paintings by Chinese masters, Thracian artefacts from Bulgaria, and a death mask of Oliver Cromwell.
(Beaumont St, Oxford OX1 2PH, www.ashmolean.org)

77. Have a Delicious Lunch at Cardiff's Riverside Market

If you find yourself in Cardiff on a sunny Sunday and you are in the mood for an al fresco lunch, the Riverside Market, which is hosted in Fiztammon Embankment every Sunday, is the place to be. More than 30 producers come to showcase their wares, so as well as buying a fresh sandwich, coffee, or pastry, you can also purchase some of the local produce such as Welsh malt whisky and farmhouse cheeses.

(Fitzhamon Embankment, Cardiff CF11 6AN, www.riversidemarket.org.uk)

78. Enjoy a Local Historic Festival, Garland Festival

England is a country full of traditions, and it's lovely to see how many of these are kept alive by local communities. One of the strangest of these traditions is the annual Garland Day, which takes place on May 29th each year in the town of Charleston in Derbyshire. The festival is said to commemorate the restoration of King Charles II in 1660 and involves the Garland King leading a procession on horseback wearing a huge and heavy flower garland down to his waist.

79. Climb Arthur's Seat for a View to Die For

You'll need some strong lungs for this one, but if you love the outdoors, this is guaranteed to be the highlight of your trip to bonny Scotland. Arthur's Seat is the main peak in Holyrood Park, a park that can be found on the outskirts of Edinburgh. It's 251 metres above sea level, allowing you to experience *the* most breath taking view of Edinburgh that can be found. It's only a 45 minute walk from the park so it makes from a memorable morning excursion that's accessible to anyone with moderate fitness.

80. Look at Stunning Art Works in the Fitzwilliam Museum

Arts lovers need to find their way to the Fitzwilliam, which is the official arts and antiquities museum of Cambridge, as a matter of priority. The selection of paintings is extremely impressive, with works from the likes of Rousseau, Rubens, and Raphael, and stunning bronzes by Michelangelo. With free admission, there's absolutely no reason not to check it out.

(32 Trumpington St, Cambridge CB2 1RB, www.fitzmuseum.cam.ac.uk)

81. Visit High Force Waterfall in the Durham Dales

There is nothing quite like standing in front of a pounding waterfall to make you appreciate all of nature's grandeur, and one of the most impressive waterfalls in England is called High Force, which can be found in the north part of the country in the Durham Dales. The water here drops with force for 21 metres, and there are many well marked trails around High Force so you can reach the waterfall with ease.

(Forest-in-Teesdale DL12 0XH, www.highforcewaterfall.com)

82. Gobble Up Haggis, Neeps, and Tatties

Okay, Scotland might not exactly be the culinary capital of Europe, but this is not to say that there are no delights to sample, and if there is one local food that you can't leave without trying, it's the famous (or should that be infamous?) haggis. Haggis is a savoury dish that comprises the heart, liver, and lungs of a sheep. These are mixed together with suet, oats, and spice, and boiled in the stomach of an animal, which it is usually served in. Errr…. delicious? And don't forget the neeps and tatties – these are the potatoes and turnips served alongside haggis.

83. Indulge an Inner Hippie at Shambala Festival

Fancy yourself as something of a hippie? Then you should consider grabbing tickets for the annual Shamabla festival, an arts and music festival that is hosted in Nottinghamshire at the end of every August. While this festival is small, it's diverse with a lot happening. You can expect rock, folk, and world music, independent film screenings, talks and debates, an organic market, and lots more fun.

(www.shambalafestival.org)

84. Go Camping in the Welsh Mountains

As you travel around Britain, you will most likely stay in hotels, guesthouses, and hostels, and while that's totally fine, a way of mixing it up a little is to have a camping experience underneath the stars. Nannerth Farm is located in the middle of Wales, and it's a traditional Welsh farm with all kinds of farm animals. They also offer a camping ground right there in the fields so you can enjoy all of this back to basics farming life in an authentic way.

(Nannerth Fawr, Rhayader LD6 5HA, www.nannerth.co.uk)

85. Spend a Day Fishing at Alderwood Ponds

If your idea of the perfect trip away doesn't involving hopping from museum to museum or visiting ancient castles but simply sitting by the edge of a lake with a fishing rod in the water, you should know about Alderwood Ponds, a fishery in West Sussex. There's a choice of three different waters here with fish like carp, perch, roach, rudd, and tench. Perhaps you'll even catch your supper.

(Horsham Rd, Steyning BN44 3AA,
https://alderwoodponds.wordpress.com)

86. Take a Sled-Dog Ride Through the Cairngorms

Although Scotland is a wonderful country to visit at any time of the year, we think that it's particularly beautiful in the winter. And if you love snow and winter sports, this is definitely the time to make your trip. Something really unique that you can do up in the snowy Cairngorm Mountains is take a sled-dog ride. If you're travelling with kids, it's something that they will particularly love, and it makes a great festive experience in the Christmas period.

87. Shop for Vintage Threads at Beyond Retro

London is one of the greatest shopping cities on the face of the earth, and the reason for this is because there are stores to cater for all budgets and all tastes. There are the high end shops on Bond Street, the high street shops all over the city, and there's also a great vintage scene, particularly in the East End. Beyond Retro have two shops in the East End, one in Dalston and one by Brick Lane, and both are incredible for finding reasonably priced vintage treasures. Sometimes they even have live music gigs inside as well.

(110-112 Cheshire St, London E2 6EJ; www.beyondretro.com)

88. Visit Wordsworth's Old Home in the Lake District

William Wordsworth was a pioneer of the Tomantic movement, and is still one of the most recognised poets from English literature. You can step back in time and actually see how the man lived by visiting his first family home, Dove Cottage, around beautiful Lake Windermere. It was in this little cottage that Wordsworth wrote some of his finest poetry, and these days it still contains his personal objects.

(Grasmere, Ambleside LA22 9SH,
https://wordsworth.org.uk/visit/dove-cottage.html)

89. Get Decadent With Afternoon Tea at The Balmoral

When you visit a new city or a new country for the first time, it's important to be a little bit indulgent, and there is nothing more British nor more indulgent than a classic afternoon tea at The Balmoral in Edinburgh. Their afternoon tea is served in a beautiful champagne bar with a glass dome and palm trees inside. You can expect all the classics such as scones with clotted cream, finger sandwiches, and, of course, pots and pots of tea.

(1 Princes St, Edinburgh EH2 2EQ;
http://balmoral.edinburgh-hotel.org)

90. Feel Floral at Columbia Road Flower Market

Market culture is something very important in London, and you can find different markets for different purposes. Columbia Road Flower Market is enduringly popular, and one of the most vibrant markets in the city. This market takes place every Sunday, and the whole city overflows with the most incredible colours, and the scents of the various flowers. As the market is in the heart of the East End, there are many options for Sunday lunch in a local pub nearby as well.

(Columbia Rd, London E2 7RG; www.columbiaroad.info)

91. Swim in the Turquoise Water of Kynance Cove

Are you looking for the most perfect beach in Britain? A place with perfectly blue waters and white sand? Then you need to make your way to Cornwall county, which in our opinion contains the best beaches in the country. There are many to choose from but Kynance Cove is extra special. This cove has incredible turquoise waters that are calm enough for swimming, and white sand where you might even be able to top up your tan on a sunny day.

(Helston TR12 7PJ)

92. Discover Cheese-Rolling on Coopers Hill

One of the strangest events that you are likely to encounter in Britain, actually the world, is the cheese rolling festival, which takes over the Spring Bank Holiday, each year, in a place called Cooper's Hill in Gloucestershire. The basic idea is that a 9lb round of Gloucestershire cheese is rolled down a hill, and local people roll themselves down the hill after it, with the first person past the finish line winning the cheese. Bonkers to say the least.

93. Feel Local History at Pembroke Castle

Great Britain is full of incredible castles, but the castle structures in England and Scotland are probably better known and more visited than those in Wales. But this is no reflection of the quality and grandeur of Welsh castles, and of the most impressive is Pembroke Castle in the west of the country. Most of the castle that remains today dates back to the 12th century, with a huge round keep, a domed roof, and a spiral stairwell connecting the four stories.

(Pembroke SA71 4LA, http://pembroke-castle.co.uk)

94. Have a Gay Night Out on Canal Street

Great Britain is an awesome place to visit if you are an LGBT traveller, and many of the cities have their very own gay streets or even districts. When you find yourself in England's second city, Manchester, the place to be for a gay night out is Canal Street. This has been a hub of gay activity since the 1980s, but it really started to flourish after it became the setting for the 1990s television drama, Queer as Folk.

(www.canal-st.co.uk)

95. Get Literary at the Annual Dickens Festival

Britain has produced some of the most iconic writers and works of literature known to man, and one of the most enduringly popular of these is Dickens, famous for incredible works like Oliver Twist, A Christmas Carol, and Great Expectations. Well, you can celebrate the great man himself at the annual Dickens Festival, which is hosted in Rochester, Kent in June. With costumed parades, street acts, readings, a fair, and more, this is the place for all bibliophiles to be.

96. Eat Incredible Fish & Chips in Plymouth

If there is one culinary dish that could be described as quintessentially British it's fish and chips. Since the country is surrounded by water, you can find great quality fish and chips all over Britain, but if you want the very best plateful, we can recommend West Hoe Fryers in Plymouth, which has won numerous awards and accolades over the years. The fish is always fresh and white, and the batter always perfectly crisp. *(7 Radford Rd, Plymouth PL1 3BY)*

97. Relax in Harrogate's Turkish Baths

When you think of places in the world to relax in an authentic Turkish bath, well, let's be honest you would probably think of Turkey before anywhere else. And who could blame you? But if you find yourself in the north of England, you'll be happy to know that there are also Turkish baths in Harrogate of all places. Turkish baths differ because they involve a process of heating, cooling, and cleansing the body.

(Royal Baths, Parliament St, Harrogate HG1 2WH,
www.turkishbathsharrogate.co.uk)

98. Get Back to Nature in Aberglasny Gardens

Ok, so there is nature all around you in Great Britain so there might not be so much of a need to "get back" to nature wherever you are, but if you would like to explore some particularly picturesque gardens while you are in Wales, Aberglasny House and Gardens could be a wonderful place to do so. You will find an Elizabethan cloister garden, 10 acres of ancient gardens, and even an indoor garden to explore.

(Aberglasney, Llangathen, Carmarthen SA32 8QH,
http://aberglasney.org)

99. Celebrate Burns' Night Like a Local

The Scots love to party, and one of the most festive nights on the Scottish calendar is Burns' Night. On Burns' Night, the Scottish population celebrates the writings of beloved Scottish poet, Robert Burns. It lands on January 25th each year, the poet's birthday, and a Haggis dinner lies at the heart of the celebration. As the haggis is brought to the table, Burns' poem, Address to a Haggis, is recited to the table of guests, who then tuck in and wash their haggis down with copious amounts of Scottish whisky.

100. Keep Kids Entertained at the Centre for Life

Keeping kids entertained on a trip away is easier said than done, but the Centre of Life in Newcastle is a place where the hours pass by in what seems like minutes, and where your kids can actually learn something while having fun. You can explore the human body in the Body World section, have a thrilling adventure on a 4D ride, and visit the north of England's largest planetarium.

(Times Square, Newcastle upon Tyne NE1 4EP; www.life.org.uk)

101. Learn All About The Beatles in Liverpool

The most famous pop group to have ever emerged from the UK, and perhaps to have emerged anywhere, is The Beatles. This four piece group found their fame in the 1960s when they started playing local clubs in Liverpool, and you can learn all about the band at The Beatles Story, a permanent exhibition dedicated to their lives and music. Inside you'll find replicas of the Casbah Club, Cavern Club, and Abbey Studios so that you feel immersed in nostalgia for the 1960s.
(Britannia Vaults, Albert Dock, Liverpool L3 4AD, www.beatlesstory.com)

Before You Go...

Thanks for reading **101 Coolest Things to Do in Great Britain.** We hope that it makes your trip a memorable one!

Keep your eyes peeled on www.101coolestthings.com, and have a wonderful trip.

Team 101 Coolest Things

Printed in Great Britain
by Amazon